BOYS, DREAMS & ADHD:
ADHD PARENTING GUIDE FOR BOYS

HANNAH MORELLA

TABLE OF CONTENT

Introduction

It can be both difficult and gratifying to raise a child with Attention Deficit Hyperactivity Disorder (ADHD). ADHD is a neurodevelopmental condition that impairs a child's capacity for concentration, impulse control, and energy management. Children with ADHD can succeed with the correct assistance and methods, despite the fact that they may face particular hurdles.

Compared to girls, boys are more likely to be diagnosed with ADHD, and they may also have different symptoms and behaviors. This parenting guide is designed to assist parents and caregivers in navigating the unique difficulties and rewards associated with raising boys who have ADHD. This book can help you whether your child has just received a diagnosis or you're looking for fresh perspectives to enhance your current parenting techniques.

We will look at the basics of ADHD in this article, covering its causes, signs, and methods of diagnosis. We will also explore doable tactics for establishing a caring and encouraging atmosphere at home. You will discover strategies to support your child's mental health, investigate opportunities for educational support, and learn how to manage behaviors associated with ADHD.

Boys with ADHD will face new chances and challenges as they enter puberty; we will talk about how to properly traverse these crucial years. We'll provide tips along the road for helping your child grow in social situations, make friends, and be ready for success in the future.

Having an ADHD child in the family calls for tolerance, understanding, and a dedication to finding the best help possible. With this handbook, we hope you will feel more equipped to appreciate your child's special qualities, provide a caring and supportive household, and speak out for their needs.

Recall that you are not traveling alone. There are numerous organizations and services available to offer assistance and direction. The first step to your child's success is your commitment to their welfare. Together, let's set out on this journey to give you the information and resources you need to support your son in thriving, embracing his uniqueness, and realizing his full potential.

Let's now start discussing ADHD and the methods that can improve your child's quality of life.

CHAPTER 1: Understanding ADHD in Boys

What is ADHD?

ADHD is a common neurodevelopmental disorder that affects people across the lifespan. It is typified by impulsivity, hyperactivity, and attention issues. Though it can affect both males and girls, boys are more likely to have ADHD than girls. Recognizing the severity of the problem and the necessity of early intervention and assistance requires an understanding of the incidence of ADHD in males.

There are three main types of ADHD:

- Predominantly inattentive presentation.
- Predominantly hyperactive/impulsive presentation.
- Combined presentation.

The basis for a diagnosis is the existence of enduring symptoms that have developed over time and become apparent during the previous six months. Although it can be identified at any age, ADHD is first identified in children. The diagnosis can only be made if the patient's symptoms have existed before the age of 12 and have created problems in multiple settings. For example, the symptoms are not limited to what happens at home.

Inattentive type

The term "inattentive" describes problems with organization, focus, and staying on task. Six (or five for those who are 17 years of age or older) of the following symptoms must regularly occur in order to be diagnosed with this kind of ADHD:

- Lacks attention to detail and carelessly completes assignments for work or education.
- Has trouble maintaining concentration on jobs or activities, such as lengthy readings, lectures, or conversations.
- Appears to be elsewhere and does not seem to listen when spoken to.
- Disregards directions and fails to finish jobs, chores, or schooling (may begin tasks but loses attention easily).
- Has trouble keeping things structured (poor time management, sloppy, disorganized work, missing deadlines, etc.).
- Avoids or detests doing anything that call for prolonged mental work, including filling out forms and writing reports.

- Frequently misplaces items that are necessary for daily living or tasks, including books, school papers, wallets, cell phones, and spectacles.
- Is prone to distractions.
- Forgets to do everyday duties like errands and chores. It's common for older adults and teens to forget to make appointments, pay bills, and return calls.

Hyperactive/impulsive type

Excessive movement, including fidgeting, having too much energy, moving about a lot, and talking a lot, is referred to as hyperactivity. Impulsivity is the term used to describe choices or acts made without considering the repercussions. Six (or five for those who are 17 years of age or older) of the following symptoms must regularly occur in order to be diagnosed with this kind of ADHD:

- Wriggles in the seat, fidgets with hands or feet, or taps them.
- Unable to remain seated (at work or in a school).
- Runs around or climbs in places that are not suitable.
- Unable to play or engage in calm leisure activities.
- Always "in motion," as though propelled by a motor.
- Talks excessively.

- Blurts out a response before the question has been fully asked (for example, finishing someone else's sentence or speaking too quickly during a conversation).
- Finds it difficult to wait for their turn, for example, when standing in line.
- Interrupts or intrudes upon others (e.g., begins utilizing other people's property without permission, or interrupts games, talks, or other activities). It's possible for older individuals and teenagers to take over tasks.

Combined type

When the criteria for both the hyperactive/impulsive and inattentive kinds of ADHD are satisfied, this type of ADHD is diagnosed.

Usually, primary care physicians or mental health professionals diagnose ADHD. A comprehensive mental and medical history, family history, information on education, surroundings, and upbringing, a description of symptoms from the patient and caregivers, and the patient, caregivers, and teachers filling out scales and questionnaires are all part of a psychiatric evaluation. In order to rule out other medical issues, it could also need a referral for medical evaluation.

It is noteworthy that a number of illnesses, including learning disabilities, mental disorders, anxiety, substance abuse, head trauma, thyroid issues, and usage of certain medications like steroids, can resemble ADHD. Additionally, oppositional defiant disorder or conduct disorder, anxiety disorders, and learning problems are among the mental health diseases that may co-occur with ADHD. Consequently, it is crucial to have a thorough mental assessment. Routine imaging or specialized blood tests are not available for the diagnosis of ADHD. In order to determine the severity of their symptoms, patients may occasionally be referred for additional psychological testing (such as neuropsychological or psychoeducational testing) or undergo computer-based assessment.

Causes of ADHD

Researchers are still working to pinpoint the exact causes of ADHD. Although a number of genes have been connected to ADHD and there is mounting evidence that heredity plays a role in the illness, no single gene or combination of genes has been found to be the primary cause of ADHD. It's crucial to remember, though, that families of those who have ADHD frequently have the same problems. There is proof that children with ADHD have brains that are anatomically different from those of children without the disorder. For example, children with ADHD show distinct brain region activity during specific tasks and have lower volume of both gray and white brain matter. According to additional research, ADHD affects the brain's frontal lobes, caudate nucleus, and cerebellar vermis. The condition has also been related to a number of non-genetic variables, including low birth weight, early birth, exposure to toxins (smoke, alcohol, lead, etc.) during pregnancy, and high levels of stress.

More Typical ADHD Symptoms in Boys

A neurodevelopmental disorder known as attention deficit hyperactivity disorder (ADHD) can present with a variety of symptoms. While each person's symptoms may differ, boys with ADHD frequently exhibit a number of common symptoms. It's crucial to keep in mind that not all guys with ADHD will show the same symptoms, and that symptoms might vary in intensity. The following are some typical signs of ADHD in boys:

1. **Inattention**:

- Inability to focus on activities or tasks for extended periods of time, especially when they're not very interesting or stimulating.

- Frequent thoughtless errors in assignments or other tasks requiring close attention to detail.
- Difficulty planning activities and tasks.
- Avoiding or vocalizing a great aversion for mental labor-intensive chores like homework.

2. Hyperactivity:

- Restlessness, trouble remaining sat, and a propensity to get up when seated is expected.
- Running or climbing when not supposed to.
- Incapacity to participate in peaceful activities.
- Talking too much.

3. Impulsivity:

- Disrupting people in sports or chats on a regular basis.
- Inability to wait one's turn during group activities.
- Rash decisions made without thinking through the repercussions.
- Entering another person's home or personal property without permission.

4. Poor Time Management:

- Having trouble managing your time and frequently being late.
- Having trouble setting priorities and finishing things in time.
- Forgetting to do tasks such as homework, housework, or other obligations.

5. Disorganization:

- A disorganized workstation, knapsack, or room.
- Often misplacing personal belongings like school supplies, books, or keys.
- Difficulty adhering to schedules and maintaining organization.

6. Academic Challenges:

- Less than one would have expected for their level of intelligence.
- Inability to turn in assignments and homework on time.
- Forgetfulness or misplacing essential school supplies.

7. Emotional Regulation:

- Intensity of emotion, such as sudden, strong rage or frustration.
- Emotional instability and fluctuations in mood.
- Less capacity to handle stress.

8. **Impaired Social Skills:**

- Inability to establish and maintain friendships with peers.
- Impulsivity that may result in social problems, including talking over other people or not sharing.

It's crucial to remember that not all boys with ADHD will show all of these signs, and that symptoms might alter as a child gets older. The symptom profile may also be impacted by co-occurring disorders like oppositional defiant disorder or anxiety. It's critical to get your son evaluated by a medical expert or mental health specialist if you think he could have ADHD in order to establish a diagnosis and create a suitable treatment plan. An early diagnosis and intervention can greatly enhance a child's academic performance and quality of life.

Diagnosis and Evaluation of ADHD in Boys

Giving boys with Attention Deficit Hyperactivity Disorder (ADHD) the care and interventions they need starts with getting an appropriate diagnosis. A thorough assessment conducted by licensed medical specialists, such as pediatricians, child psychologists, or child psychiatrists, is usually the first step in the diagnosis procedure. An outline of the diagnosis and assessment procedure is provided below:

1. First Evaluation:

Parent and Teacher Input: Gathering data from parents and teachers is frequently the first step in the process. They could be required to fill out checklists or questionnaires regarding the behavior of the child, with an emphasis on symptoms associated with ADHD.

Medical History: In order to rule out any possible explanations for the child's symptoms, a complete medical history is necessary. It's critical to share details regarding the child's developmental history, any prior medical illnesses or medication history, and the family history of ADHD.

2. Medical Consultation:

To learn more about the child's behavior, feelings, and general functioning, the medical expert will interview the parents and child in a clinical setting. A wide range of subjects, such as daily routines, academic achievement, and family dynamics, may be discussed during this interview.

3. ADHD Standards:

The child's symptoms must match certain criteria listed in the Diagnostic and Statistical Manual of Mental Disorders (DSM-5), a widely used diagnostic guide for mental health disorders, in order for the child to be officially diagnosed with ADHD. These requirements include impulsivity, hyperactivity, and inattentional symptoms.

4. Behavior Assessment and Rating Scales:

The child's behavior can be evaluated using standardized rating scales and behavior evaluations, and it can be compared to usual developmental norms. These instruments facilitate the measurement and evaluation of ADHD symptom severity.

5. Eliminate Co-Occurring Conditions:

It's critical to rule out the existence of co-occurring disorders like anxiety, depression, or learning difficulties that could accompany ADHD. Occasionally, these disorders may mimic or worsen symptoms of ADHD.

6. Academic Documents:

Report cards and teacher observations, among other school documents, are excellent resources for learning about a child's conduct and academic standing. Working together with the child's school can help shed light on how ADHD affects behavior and learning in a classroom environment.

7. Taking note:

Confirmation of the existence of ADHD symptoms and their influence on day-to-day living can be achieved by observing the child's behavior in several contexts, including home and school.

8. All-encompassing Evaluation:

An extensive evaluation that considers all relevant data is usually used to make the diagnosis of ADHD. A licensed healthcare provider with experience diagnosing ADHD should make the diagnosis.

9. Creating a Plan of Treatment:

Following diagnosis, the medical practitioner will collaborate with the child's parents to create a personalized treatment plan. A mix of interventions, including behavioral therapy, medication, and educational assistance, may be part of this plan.

10. Continuous Observation:

Since ADHD is a chronic illness, it is imperative to evaluate a child's progress and modify the treatment plan as needed throughout their lifetime. It's critical to keep lines of communication open and schedule follow-up meetings with healthcare specialists.

CHAPTER 2: Nurturing a Positive Environment

Creating a Supportive Home for a Child with ADHD

There are benefits and challenges associated with being a parent of a kid with attention deficit hyperactivity disorder (ADHD). Creating a supportive home environment is essential to fostering your child's growth and assisting them in overcoming any challenges that ADHD may bring. Your child can gain resilience, self-worth, and important life skills from a loving and orderly environment. These are the main techniques for setting up a nurturing environment in the home for an ADHD child:

1. Recognizing ADHD: It's critical to recognize ADHD in order to have a supportive home. ADHD is a neurodevelopmental disorder that impacts a child's ability to control their attention, impulses, and activity levels. It is not the result of being lazy or lacking self-discipline. Acknowledging ADHD as a legitimate and treatable disorder will help you deal with your child's difficulties patiently and empathetically.

2. Clear Communication: The foundation of any supportive home is effective communication. Discuss ADHD with your child, using language that is suitable for their age. Invite them to share their thoughts and worries. Your child can feel heard and understood when there is open and safe communication.

3. Establish Routines: Structured routines are often beneficial for children with ADHD. A regular daily routine can provide your child a feeling of consistency and improve how well they manage their time and responsibilities. To keep your youngster organized, make a visual schedule for them to follow using charts or apps.

4. Break Up the Tasks into Smaller Steps: A youngster with ADHD may find it difficult to complete tasks that appear straightforward to others. Assign work to smaller, more achievable segments and give precise directions. Acknowledge and acknowledge their progress to increase their self-confidence.

5. Arrange the surroundings: Your youngster will be able to concentrate better and have fewer distractions in an orderly, clutter-free environment. Set apart particular areas for play, relaxation, and homework. Label products and use storage solutions to keep things where they belong.

6. Promote Independence: Encourage your youngster to accept age-appropriate responsibilities to foster independence. Allowing children to exercise decision-making authority promotes self-reliance and self-assurance. Nonetheless, offer tactful direction and oversight as required.

7. Promote Physical Activity: Children with ADHD need to engage in regular physical activity. It helps individuals release pent-up energy, sharpen focus, and elevate mood. Promote sports, outdoor play, and other physical activities your youngster finds enjoyable.

8. Limit Screen Time: Children with ADHD may suffer from excessive screen time. Limit the amount of time spent on screens while promoting reading, hobbies, and imaginative play.

9. Positive Reinforcement: Encourage and recognize your child's efforts and accomplishments by using positive reinforcement. Give them credit for any success, no matter how tiny, and set up a reward system that promotes positive behavior.

10. Empathy and Patience: Raising an ADHD child might be difficult, but it's important to handle their challenges with empathy and patience. Recognize that they might have trouble controlling their emotions and impulses. Provide them with affection and encouragement, and assist them in creating coping mechanisms during trying times.

A child with ADHD needs a supportive environment at home, which calls for commitment and flexibility. You may help your child develop critical life skills and confidence by creating a regulated, empathetic, and loving environment. This will help them thrive despite the difficulties presented by ADHD. Keep in mind that each child is different, and as your family continues to learn and develop together, what works best for you may change over time.

Establishing Routine and Structure

For a youngster diagnosed with Attention Deficit Hyperactivity Disorder (ADHD), it is critical to establish a daily schedule and structure. Children with ADHD may find it difficult to organize themselves, control their impulses, and manage their time. Nonetheless, a regimen that is well-organized can offer the consistency and dependability young kids require to flourish. Here, we explore the value of regularity and structure and provide advice on how to create and preserve them.

The Value of Structure and Routine

The executive functions of a child, which include impulse control, time management, and organization, are frequently problematic for kids with ADHD. These problems can be made worse by a lack of structure and regularity, which can make the family and the child feel stressed and chaotic. A consistent schedule has numerous important advantages:

- Predictability: Children with ADHD may find comfort in the predictability of a regular schedule. Anxiety is lessened and transitions between activities are easier when people know what to expect from their day.

- Time management: Children who follow a routine are better able to manage their time. They are able to comprehend the passage of time and learn how to divide it up across different tasks.

- Organization: Regular structure promotes organization. Youngsters pick up organizing skills, task prioritization, and day-planning knowledge.

- Task Completion: Children are better able to concentrate on and finish tasks when they follow a routine. They are aware of when chores, homework, and other obligations are due.

- Decreased Decision-Making: Regular activities help to reduce the demand for ongoing decision-making. Children can save their mental energy for other tasks when they are aware of what is required of them at different times.

- Stress Reduction: A regimen that is well-organized helps the family and the child feel less stressed and anxious. It gets rid of the confusion that disorganization and impulsive actions frequently bring.

Putting Structure and Routine in Place

A youngster with ADHD needs careful planning and patience while developing a regimen. The following actions can assist you in creating a regimented daily schedule:

- Work Together with Your Child: Allow your child to participate in the routine's creation. Talk about the schedule while taking their needs and preferences into account. Children are more inclined to follow routines when they have a say in them.

- Regular Bedtime and Wake-Up Times: Establish regular bedtime and wake-up times right away. Maintaining a regular sleep schedule is essential for both mood management and cognitive performance.

- Visual Schedules: To depict the daily routine, use visual aids like charts or whiteboards. Children with ADHD find it easier to comprehend and adhere to visual routines.

- Time Blocks: Assign time slots to each day that correspond to distinct activities. Set aside a block, for instance, for bedtime, playing, schoolwork, and breakfast. Specify times for transitioning between each activity.

- Have Realistic Expectations: Be honest with yourself about what can be completed in the time allotted. Routine flexibility and breaks are important since inflexibility can cause frustration.

- Incorporate Important Activities: Make sure the schedule includes important things like housework, homework, meals, exercise, and relaxation time.

- Make Use of Timers and Alarms: Children can benefit from timers and alarms as they go from one task to the next. An aural and visual indication can be provided by setting a timer for the beginning and finish of tasks.

- Have Patience and Flexibility: Keep in mind that creating a habit takes time. Remain calm and adaptable, and be ready to change the routine as necessary. It is important to modify the routine according to your child's individual requirements and preferences because what works for one child might not work for another.

- Give Praise and Reinforcement: Congratulate your youngster on following the routine and acknowledge their efforts. Rewarding behavior can encourage them to stick to their plan.

- Seek Professional Guidance: If you're having trouble creating or sticking to a schedule, think about consulting a therapist or medical professional who has experience working with ADHD kids. They are able to offer customized tactics and assistance.

For a child with ADHD, establishing a disciplined schedule can have a big impact on their everyday lives. It eases tension, fosters the growth of critical life skills, and offers a sense of stability and security. Together, you and your child may create a routine that supports their achievement and well-being by being patient and adaptable.

Setting Realistic Expectations for a Child with ADHD

Managing your child's symptoms and assisting them in succeeding in different areas of life is one of the special challenges that come with being a parent of an ADHD child. Setting reasonable expectations is essential to

being a good parent of an ADHD child. By doing this,
you can lessen irritation, raise your child's
self-confidence, and foster an environment that is
conducive to their development. Here's how to give an
ADHD youngster reasonable expectations:

1. Recognize ADHD: It's important to recognize
    ADHD before establishing expectations. Realize
    that your child has a neurodevelopmental
    condition that interferes with their ability to focus,
    control their impulses, and behave appropriately.
    You can better set expectations for them if you
    understand the nature of ADHD and take into
    consideration their limitations.

2. Individualized Approach: A customized
    approach is necessary as each child with ADHD
    is different and what suits one may not suit
    another. Adjust your expectations based on your
    child's unique requirements, abilities, and
    constraints. Take into account their age, stage of
    development, and symptom intensity.

3. Keep Your Eye on Progress, Not Perfection: It's
    critical to keep in mind that any advancement, no
    matter how tiny, counts as a victory. Rather from
    placing unrealistic expectations on your
    youngster, emphasize their efforts and growth.
    No matter how small their victories may be,
    acknowledge them.

4. Break Tasks Into Manageable Steps: Children with ADHD may find it difficult to handle complex tasks. Divide them into more manageable, smaller steps. Your youngster will find it simpler to finish assignments and experience a sense of success as a result.

5. Establish Clear, Specific Goals: Be clear about the outcomes you want your child to attain when establishing expectations. Provide examples and express your requirements in plain language. stating something like, "Do your homework," as an example, would be better than stating, "Complete one math problem before taking a short break."

6. Provide Consistency and Structure: Create a regimen and follow it. Being consistent eases the anxiety that comes with being unpredictable for kids with ADHD.

7. Have a Realistic Perspective on Attention Spans: Recognize that kids with ADHD could have shorter attention spans than their classmates. Assign responsibilities appropriately, and when needed, schedule regular pauses.

8. Refrain from Overcommitting Your Child to Too Many Activities: While it's important for kids to participate in a variety of activities, try not to overcommit your child. Give top priority to

activities that fit their strengths and areas of interest.

9. Promote Self-Advocacy: Help your youngster learn how to express their demands and stand up for themselves. This is a useful skill in the classroom and other situations where they might need extra help or modifications.

10. Control Expectations at School: Work with your child's teachers to make sure that the standards they set for their academic performance are realistic and appropriate for their level of ability. They can have their educational experience customized to meet their unique requirements with the use of a 504 Plan or an Individualized Education Plan (IEP).

11. Use Positive Reinforcement: You can encourage your child to meet your expectations by providing them with praise and rewards. To increase their self-esteem and confidence, acknowledge their efforts and accomplishments.

12. Seek Professional Guidance: If you struggle to manage or set expectations, you might want to speak with a therapist who has worked with ADHD patients or a mental health professional. They can provide tips and direction on how to deal with the particular difficulties of raising an ADHD child.

It takes time, patience, flexibility, and understanding to set reasonable expectations for a child with ADHD. You may help your child succeed by understanding their individual talents and difficulties and by creating a safe, orderly environment for them to grow in. Recall that your understanding and support are crucial to their success and well-being.

Encouraging Independence in Children with ADHD

One of the most important things for parents to do when raising a child with Attention Deficit Hyperactivity Disorder (ADHD) is to support their independence. Even though attention, organization, and impulse control can be challenging for children with ADHD, it's important to encourage your child's independence and self-reliance. The following are some methods to help kids with ADHD become more independent:

1. Give Your Child Clear directions: Get started by providing your child with precise directions. Processing multiple pieces of information at once is a common challenge for kids with ADHD. Divide work into smaller, more doable segments and make sure your directions are clear.

2.	Visual Supports: Using visual aids to encourage independence can be quite effective. To assist your child in understanding and adhering to routines, assignments, and responsibilities, use visual schedules, charts, and checklists. These illustrations offer a feeling of order and dependability.

3.	Teach Organizational Skills: Teaching organizational skills to kids with ADHD can be very beneficial. Show them how to establish to-do lists, maintain an ordered home, and develop and utilize a calendar. As kids practice these abilities, be patient and provide guidance.

4.	Promote Self-Advocacy: Give your kids the tools they need to stand up for themselves. Teach kids to express their wants and difficulties to parents, instructors, and peers alike. This is a very useful skill in both social and academic situations.

5.	Tools for Time Management: Assist your youngster in learning time management techniques. Show them how to efficiently manage their time and stay on task by introducing them to tools like timers and alerts. These resources can be very helpful while switching between tasks.

6.	Set Reasonable Expectations: It's important to set reasonable expectations while promoting independence. Acknowledge the skills and limitations of your child and modify your expectations accordingly. Prioritize progress over perfection.

7. Encourage Making Decisions:Give your kids the freedom to choose within developmentally acceptable bounds. Encourage children to select their own clothes, snacks, and pastimes. They can hone their decision-making abilities by making these choices.

8. Promote Problem-Solving: Instruct your kids on problem-solving methods. Help them come up with ideas and make decisions to get beyond hurdles when they face difficulties or setbacks.

9. Praise Little Achievements and Efforts: Give your kids credit for their efforts and minor triumphs. They feel more confident and are inspired to take on more duties when they receive positive reinforcement.

10. Gradual Independence: Promote independence in a methodical, gradual way. As they gain confidence and competence, start with easy tasks and progressively increase their level of responsibility.

11. Seek Professional Assistance: Take into account obtaining assistance from therapists or mental

health specialists who specialize in treating ADHD. They can provide methods and treatments that are customized to your child's particular requirements, encouraging independence in a controlled and encouraging way.

12. Find the Correct Balance between Supervision and Freedom: It's critical to find the ideal balance between supervision and freedom. Give your child some independence as long as you are there to supervise them appropriately. They can develop responsibility and learn from their mistakes with the aid of this method.

13. Show Patience and Support: Promoting independence requires both patience and encouragement. For children with ADHD, learning new skills and tasks may take longer and require more practice. Encourage and reassure others by being there.

A compassionate and sympathetic attitude is necessary to help a youngster with ADHD develop independence. You can assist your child in gaining the confidence and independence necessary to successfully navigate everyday challenges by teaching them important life skills, providing guidance, and acknowledging their accomplishments. It is crucial for you to be a helpful parent in order to foster their development and independence.

Effective Communication for Boys with ADHD

Parenting requires effective communication, and this is especially true when your child has Attention Deficit Hyperactivity Disorder (ADHD). A youngster with ADHD may have trouble focusing, controlling their impulses, and processing information, which can occasionally lead to communication difficulties. The following techniques will assist you in having productive conversations with your ADHD child:

1. Listening Intently: Pay attention to what your youngster is saying. When they are speaking, give them your whole attention and keep looking them in the eye. Express your appreciation for their ideas and perspectives.

2. Employ Simple and Clear terminology: Be direct and succinct in your terminology. Steer clear of long or complicated sentences. When giving directions or making requests, be clear so that your child knows exactly what is expected of them.

3. Give One Instruction at a Time: Kids with ADHD could find it challenging to process more than

one instruction at once. Divide assignments or instructions into more manageable chunks. Give them one assignment to finish before moving on to the next.

4. Keep a Positive Tone: When speaking with your youngster, keep your tone upbeat and encouraging. Refrain from being unduly harsh or negative. Rewarding behavior can inspire people and boost their self-esteem.

5. Make Use of Visual Aids: Graphics like charts, graphs, and drawings can be very beneficial. They provide knowledge and a visual representation, which helps your child comprehend and retain it.

6. Establish a Structured Setting:Establish a disciplined, well-organized atmosphere that facilitates efficient communication. Reduce uncertainty and increase predictability by implementing routines and visual schedules.

7. Ask Open-Ended Questions: Promote discourse by posing open-ended questions that don't just accept a "yes" or "no" answer. This encourages dialogue and facilitates your child's more complete self-expression.

8. Respect Their Viewpoint: Even if your child's viewpoint is different from your own,

acknowledge and value it. Encourage them to share their ideas and opinions, and give them permission to experience what they are feeling.

9. Have patience and give them time to digest information: Kids with ADHD might require extra time to think things through and react. Before anticipating a response, exercise patience and give them enough time to gather their ideas.

10. Nonverbal Communication: Be aware of your own body language. Important information can be communicated by gestures, body language, and facial expressions. To demonstrate that you are open to hearing what your child has to say, keep your posture open and kind.

11. Deal with One conduct at a Time: Pay attention to one particular conduct at a time while talking about behavioral concerns. Don't give your child a long list of worries to worry about. Make sure you understand the behavior you wish to change and its significance.

12. Use Positive Reinforcement: Congratulate your child on their efforts and achievements by giving them praise and positive reinforcement. These encouraging comments may inspire them to keep up the desired habits.

13. Preserve Calm: Make an effort to foster a relaxed and stress-free atmosphere for dialogue. Steer clear of loud voices and strong emotional outbursts, as these can overwhelm kids with ADHD.

14. Seek Professional Support: If you run into communication difficulties that don't seem to go away, think about getting advice from a therapist or mental health professional who has expertise working with kids who have ADHD. They can provide particular tactics to help your family communicate better.

Being able to communicate well with your child can help them flourish and foster a healthy parent-child bond.

CHAPTER 3: Strategies for Managing ADHD

Medication Options for ADHD

One of the most popular and successful therapies for children's Attention Deficit Hyperactivity Disorder (ADHD) is medication. Medication for ADHD aims to help control the main symptoms of the disorder, such as impulsivity, hyperactivity, and inattention. While not appropriate for every child with ADHD, medication can be a useful component of an all-encompassing treatment strategy when given and closely supervised by medical specialists.

Pharmacological Stimulants:

The most widely used and extensively studied therapies for ADHD are stimulant drugs. They function by raising the brain's concentrations of specific neurotransmitters, such as norepinephrine and dopamine. These drugs have the potential to greatly reduce hyperactivity, impulsive control, and poor focus. Several stimulant drugs that are frequently administered include:

- Methylphenidate-based drugs: Quillivant XR, Ritalin, Concerta, and Metadate are a few examples.

- Medication based on amphetamines: Adderall, Adderall XR, Vyvanse, and Dexedrine are examples of these.

Typically, stimulant drugs come in a variety of forms, such as extended-release and short-acting formulations. The unique demands of the kid and the amount of time needed for symptom control throughout the day determine the choice of medication and formulation.

Non-Stimulating Drugs:

Non-stimulant drugs may be considered in situations where stimulants are not helpful, are poorly tolerated, or raise concerns about possible side effects. While these drugs don't function the same way as stimulants, they can still be useful in treating ADHD symptoms. Among the non-stimulant drugs are:

- Atomoxetine, often known as strattera, is a non-stimulant that affects the brain's norepinephrine levels. It might not start working completely for a few weeks.

- Two alpha-2 adrenergic agonists that can aid with hyperactivity and impulsivity are guanfacine

(Intuniv) and clonidine (Kapvay). They are occasionally used with stimulants.

Selecting the Appropriate Drug:

A child's unique needs, medical history, and specific symptoms should all be taken into consideration when choosing the best medicine for an ADHD youngster. When prescribing ADHD drugs, medical practitioners frequently take the following factors into account:

- Symptom Presentation: A child's main ADHD symptoms, such as impulsivity, hyperactivity, and inattention, can affect which medication is prescribed.

- Reaction to Prior Medication: If a child has taken ADHD medication in the past, the efficacy and side effects of those treatments may influence the choice of new ones.

- Possible Side Effects: Choosing a medication may be influenced by the likelihood of specific side effects or by the existence of comorbid conditions.

- Duration of Effect: Whether short-acting or extended-release formulations are more suited depends on the child's daily routine, school schedule, and activity level.

Observation and Modification:

It is crucial to keep a close eye on the child's response to medication and any possible adverse effects as soon as one is prescribed. Usually, medical professionals would alter a patient's dosage as necessary to get the best possible balance between managing symptoms and minimizing side effects. To evaluate growth and answer any worries or inquiries from the kid or parents, follow-up sessions on a regular basis are essential.

It's crucial to remember that, although medication can be a very useful tool in treating ADHD symptoms, it often works best when incorporated into a thorough treatment program. To meet a kid with ADHD's larger requirements, behavioral therapy, educational assistance, and lifestyle interventions should be taken into account.

In the end, parents, medical professionals, and, in some situations, the child themselves should collaborate in deciding whether to utilize medication to treat ADHD. Children with ADHD can significantly improve their daily functioning and general quality of life with the right medication, appropriate monitoring, and a comprehensive approach to therapy.

Behavioral Therapy for Children with ADHD

Therapy for Childhood ADHD

Your child's doctor will likely suggest behavior therapy as a treatment if attention deficit hyperactivity disorder (ADHD) has been identified in them.

Experts say it's the first step to successfully treating your child's ADHD symptoms, regardless of their age.

Behavioral therapy differs from both play therapy and psychotherapy. It emphasizes behavior over feelings. It can instruct your child on how to transform disruptive, negative energy into constructive ideas and deeds. And as the parent, it begins with you at home.

Additionally, behavioral therapy is not the same as occupational therapy or ADHD coaching. While they could be a valuable asset to your child's team for certain objectives, ADHD coaches are neither physicians nor therapists. Occupational therapy aids in developing abilities for everyday jobs.

When to Get Started

Generally speaking, behavioral therapy is advised by doctors as soon as your child receives an ADHD diagnosis. When a child is diagnosed in preschool (at the age of four or five), this is typically the only course of treatment. Research indicates that for young children, behavioral therapy is just as effective as medication. Your preschooler's doctor may recommend medication if they don't improve or if they have moderate to severe symptoms.

For children six years of age and up, the American Academy of Pediatrics (AAP) suggests behavioral therapy in addition to medicine. The term "multimodal approach" is occasionally used to describe the combined treatment. Play therapy is a technique used by some therapists with young children to help them express their feelings and experiences via play. However, the CDC notes that research has not demonstrated that talk therapy or play therapy reduces the symptoms of ADHD in young children.

Parent Training

The adults parenting the child typically the parent or parents are the primary caregivers for behavioral treatment. The techniques and abilities they'll need for this activity are taught to them throughout parent education.

The only form of therapy that the CDC suggests for young children with ADHD is parent training. Typically, a parent will see a therapist for at least eight sessions to learn the methods they'll need as well as to receive support and feedback.

Parents might benefit from stress management education as well. It can assist you in learning how to maintain your composure when your child's ADHD symptoms are upsetting you.

Teachers and other caregivers who spend time with your child also provide assistance. The goal is to surround your child with strong role models who will regularly and effectively reward good conduct and discourage bad behavior.

How to Commence

You do not need to see a specialist counselor, however some parents opt for an ADHD behavioral therapist. Parents can receive training in ADHD behavior therapy through classes. Find out from your child's physician if there are any local classes offered. Occasionally, they are included under titles like:

- ❖ Behavioral management training for parents
- ❖ Behavioral parent training
- ❖ Parent behavior training
- ❖ Parent training

You learn from a therapist in class how to establish and enforce rules and how to deal with the actions of ADHD patients. Typically, classes meet once a week for three to four months. According to research, this training will improve your relationship with your child in addition to helping you both stop their bad conduct.

Goals of Treatment

It's common for kids with ADHD to have difficulty staying still. They might be impetuous and restless. They may find it challenging to concentrate their attention as a result. It may also cause disruptions at home and in the classroom. Through behavioral treatment, your child can learn helpful skills. These:

- ❖ Bolster positive behavior
- ❖ Restrict disruptive actions
- ❖ Teach a child how to calmly communicate their emotions.

Three fundamental steps are taken first:

- Give your child a specific objective. Be realistic and precise. Ensure that your youngster knows what is expected of them. For instance, finish a homework assignment by a specific deadline.
- Be dependable when it comes to incentives and penalties. Reward your youngster whenever they behave well. Ensure that they are aware of the

repercussions for misbehaving. and see it through to the end.
- For the duration of their childhood, consistently apply the rewards/penalties system. By doing this, positive behavior develops.

Particular methods used in behavioral therapy consist of:

- Encouragement that is positive: Give your kid a reward for good conduct. Example: You can play a video game if you complete your assignment correctly and on time.
- Economics of tokens: This integrates the concepts of consequence and reward. This approach is frequently employed by teachers by assigning star stickers, but the same idea should be applied at home as well.
- Reaction expense: Rewards or privileges are taken away as a result of unwanted behavior. As an illustration, you forfeit online time if you neglect your schoolwork.
- Pause now: This standard punishment is frequently applied to preschoolers who exhibit misbehaving. For instance, you have to spend some time sitting silently by yourself if you hit your sister.

Alternative and Complementary Treatments for ADHD

For children with Attention Deficit Hyperactivity Disorder (ADHD), some parents and caregivers look into complementary and alternative therapies in addition to traditional ones like behavioral therapy and medication. These non-traditional methods, which may or may not have scientific backing, are frequently taken into account in addition to conventional therapies. It is imperative that you seek advice from medical specialists before attempting any alternative treatments to make sure your child is safe and suitable for them. The following are some complementary and alternative approaches that have been thought of for treating ADHD:

1. Dietary Interventions: A few parents have experimented with dietary adjustments for their kids, like removing specific additives, preservatives, or artificial coloring from their meals. Certain food ingredients may cause allergies in certain children with ADHD, despite the conflicting scientific evidence in favor of dietary therapy. For advice on dietary modifications, speak with a licensed dietitian or nutritionist.

2.   Omega-3 Fatty Acids: Research has looked into the possibility of using omega-3 fatty acids, which are present in fish oil and a few other foods, to help treat the symptoms of ADHD. According to certain studies, some youngsters may benefit slightly from taking omega-3 supplements in terms of their conduct and attention.

3.   Herbal Remedies: Ginkgo biloba and ginseng supplements have been investigated as possible herbal remedies for ADHD. Nevertheless, there is little data to support their efficacy, and it is unclear whether or not youngsters should take them safely or at the recommended dosages.

4.   Neurofeedback: This kind of biofeedback teaches people how to control their brain activity. It has been investigated as an ADHD remedy. Although some studies point to possible advantages, more investigation is required to prove its effectiveness.

5.   Mindfulness and Yoga: For kids with ADHD, mindfulness exercises and yoga have been suggested as complementary therapies. These methods could enhance stress reduction, emotional control, and focus. The integration of mindfulness-based therapies into behavioral therapy is common.

6. Homeopathy: As an alternate treatment for ADHD, some people have resorted to homeopathic treatments. The safety and effectiveness of homeopathic medications can be a worry, though, as there is little scientific evidence to support the effectiveness of homeopathy.

7. Chiropractic Care: Although there may be safety concerns and a lack of solid scientific data, chiropractic adjustments have been investigated as an alternative treatment for ADHD.

8. Acupuncture: This traditional Chinese medicine involves inserting tiny needles into predetermined bodily locations. Acupuncture is generally regarded as safe, however there is little data regarding its effectiveness in treating ADHD.

9. Exercise and Physical Activity: Engaging in regular physical activity helps improve mood and focus as well as general well-being. As part of an ADHD treatment strategy, encouraging your child to participate in physical activities they enjoy might be beneficial.

10. Environmental Modifications: Reducing sensory inputs in the classroom or at home can help make the environment more conducive to the needs of children with ADHD.

11. Parenting Skills Training: To help their child with ADHD more effectively, some parents find that they benefit from training in behavioral management and parenting techniques. These programs can provide methods and approaches for dealing with difficult behaviors.

You should speak with a physician or other healthcare expert who specializes in ADHD before looking into complementary or alternative therapies. They can advise you on the possible efficacy and safety of various methods as well as assist you in choosing the best course of action for your child. To make sure that all therapies, conventional and alternative, are coordinated and tailored to your child's individual needs, it's also imperative that you stay in constant communication with your child's medical team.

Diet and Nutrition for Children with ADHD

Children's overall health, especially that of those with Attention Deficit Hyperactivity Disorder (ADHD), is greatly influenced by diet and nutrition. Even while there isn't a single diet that works for everyone when it comes to treating ADHD, there are some dietary decisions and tactics that can help with symptom management and general wellness. The following factors should be taken into account when maximizing nutrition and diet for kids with ADHD:

1. Balanced Diet: Stress the need of eating a varied range of nutrient-rich foods from all food groups in a balanced diet. The general health and cognitive development of your child can be enhanced by feeding them a diet high in fruits, vegetables, whole grains, lean meats, and healthy fats.

2. Protein: Providing enough protein in your child's diet will assist control blood sugar levels and promote long-lasting energy. Lean meats, poultry, fish, dairy products, eggs, legumes, and nuts are all excellent sources of protein.

3. Omega-3 Fatty Acids: Research has indicated that omega-3 fatty acids, which are present in walnuts, flaxseeds, chia seeds, and fatty fish like salmon and trout, may be helpful in reducing the symptoms of ADHD. Think about introducing these foods into your child's diet, or ask a doctor about omega-3 supplements.

4. Whole Grains: Whole grains help control blood sugar levels and offer a consistent energy source. When preparing your child's meals, use whole grains such as brown rice, whole wheat pasta, and whole grain bread.

5. Eat Less Sugar and Processed Foods: Eating a lot of sugar-filled and highly processed food can cause energy surges and crashes, which can make symptoms of ADHD worse. Reduce your intake of highly processed foods, sugary drinks, and sugary snacks.

6. Hydration: Make sure your youngster drinks enough water throughout the day to keep properly hydrated. Dehydration can impair mood and cognitive function.

7. Meal and Snack Timing: Set aside specified periods for meals and snacks. By following this regimen, your child's day will become more predictable and their blood sugar levels will be stabilized.

8. Food Additives and Preservatives: A number of parents and guardians decide to remove artificial flavors, colors, and preservatives from their child's food. Even though there is conflicting scientific data on this issue, it can be something to think about if you think your child may be sensitive to these substances.

9. Caffeine and High-Energy Drinks: Restrict your child's intake of caffeinated and high-energy drinks because they can worsen impulsivity and hyperactivity and interfere with sleep.

10. Tailored Approach: Keep in mind that every child
     with ADHD is different, and what suits one might
     not suit another. Observe how your youngster
     reacts differently to various foods and dietary
     options. Maintain a food journal to monitor any
     patterns or possible triggers.

Speak with a Healthcare Professional:
 It's crucial to speak with a pediatrician, registered
dietitian, or other healthcare provider who specializes in
both nutrition and ADHD. Based on your child's unique
requirements, preferences, and any dietary restrictions
or allergies, they can offer tailored advice and nutritional
suggestions.

Dietary supplements and elimination diets:
Using dietary supplements or restricted diets (like
elimination diets) to treat ADHD should be done so
carefully and under a doctor's supervision. Even while
some kids might benefit from particular supplements or
dietary adjustments, it's crucial to make sure that these
interventions are safe and appropriate for your child's
general health and dietary requirements.

All things considered, a healthy, well-balanced diet
together with additional therapies like behavioral therapy
and medication can help children with ADHD manage
their symptoms better and feel better overall. Keeping a
close eye on your child's food choices and maintaining

regular contact with medical specialists will help maximize their nutritional support.

The Importance of Sleep and Exercise for Children with ADHD

Children, especially those with Attention Deficit Hyperactivity Disorder (ADHD), benefit greatly from sleep and exercise, two essential elements of a balanced lifestyle. Setting aside time for regular exercise and enough sleep can be very important for controlling the symptoms of ADHD and improving general health. For kids with ADHD, sleep and exercise are crucial for the following reasons:

Sleep:

- Cognitive Function: To maintain the best possible cognitive function, one must get enough sleep. Children with ADHD benefit from sleep in terms of improved focus, memory, and decision-making skills.

- Sleep has a critical role in emotional regulation. Kids who get enough sleep are more adept at controlling their feelings and handling pressure and annoyance.

- Hyperactivity and Impulsivity: Two of the main symptoms of ADHD, hyperactivity and impulsivity, can be made worse by sleep deprivation. Children who get enough sleep are better able to control their urges and use less excessive energy.

- Better Attention: Sleep promotes increased focus and attention, which helps kids stay on task and finish it more successfully.

- Behavior Control: Getting enough sleep can result in better behavioral control, which is crucial for kids with ADHD. It lessens disruptive behaviors and impulsive acts.

Suggestions for Encouraging Sound Sleep:

- Set up a consistent sleep pattern that includes a bedtime and wake-up time.
- Establish a soothing nighttime ritual to let the body know when it's time to relax.
- Make sure your room is quiet, dark, and cold to create a good sleeping environment.
- Reduce your time spent in front of displays (TV, PC, smartphones) an hour before bed because blue light from screens can disrupt your sleep.
- In the afternoon and evening, in particular, watch your caffeine intake.

Exercise:

- Increased Focus and Concentration: Research has indicated that engaging in physical activity enhances attention, focus, and concentration. Children with ADHD can stay on task and finish homework more quickly with regular exercise.

- Emotional Control: Physical activity triggers the production of endorphins, which naturally elevate mood. This can lessen tension and anxiety in kids and help them better control their emotions.

- Energy Expenditure: Engaging in physical activity gives youngsters with ADHD a way to let off steam and curb their impulsive and restless tendencies.

- Better Sleep: As previously mentioned, regular exercise helps enhance the quality of sleep, which is especially important for kids with ADHD.

- Social Interaction: Playing sports or group activities can help with self-esteem, social skills, and opportunity for constructive peer interaction.

Advice for Promoting Frequent Exercise:

- Find your child's favorite physical activity, be it swimming, dancing, team sports, or outdoor play.
- Make physical activity a habit, trying to get in at least 60 minutes a day most days of the week.

- Engage in physical activities with the entire family to foster a welcoming and supportive atmosphere.
- Encourage your child to engage in imaginative and unstructured outdoor play to help them let off steam.

Remember:

While exercise and sleep are important for kids with ADHD, it's also important to speak with pediatricians and other medical professionals to create a comprehensive treatment plan that is suited to your child's individual needs. This strategy may involve a mix of medication, behavioral therapy, dietary modifications, exercise, and sleep to support your child's overall health and effectively manage symptoms of ADHD.

CHAPTER 4: Educational Support

Working with School

One of the most important parts of treating children with Attention Deficit Hyperactivity Disorder (ADHD) efficiently is collaborating with schools. A helpful atmosphere for your child's social and academic development can be created by working together with teachers and school personnel. When your child has ADHD, keep the following points in mind when working with schools:

1. Open Communication: Keep lines of communication open and consistent with your child's educators, school counselor, and other pertinent personnel. Tell them about your child's ADHD diagnosis and any pertinent details, such as their strengths and weaknesses. By working together, the school and home can better meet your child's needs.

2. Create a 504 or Individualized Education Plan (IEP): Take into consideration collaborating with the school to create a 504 or Individualized Education Plan (IEP). The plans delineate particular accommodations, changes, and support services that your kid might require in order to achieve academic success. These may consist of extra time for homework and exams, first choice of seats, and assistive technology availability.

3. Educate School Staff: Give educators and other staff members resources and information regarding ADHD. By having a greater understanding of ADHD, its effects on behavior and learning, and evidence-based management techniques, educators can help your kid more effectively.

4. Set Reasonable Expectations: Work with educators to help your child's expectations be reasonable. A youngster with ADHD may struggle to finish assignments, maintain organization, and manage their time. Your child's confidence can grow and frustration can be decreased by setting realistic expectations and goals.

5. Regular Progress Monitoring: Attend parent-teacher conferences and ask the school for updates to stay up to date on your child's academic progress. Regular monitoring enables you to quickly resolve any problems and modify the support plan as necessary.

6. Assistance with Homework and Organization: Collaborate with educators to guarantee that your offspring obtains assistance with homework and organization. This can involve using checklists, assignment diaries, and explicit directions. Assist your child in creating a calm, well-organized study area at home as well as a homework schedule.

7. Medication Administration: If your kid takes ADHD medication, talk to the principal and school nurse about how to administer the medicine during school hours. Make sure all required authorizations and papers are in order.

8. Social and Emotional assistance: Suggest that your child receive social and emotional assistance. This can entail taking part in peer support initiatives, counseling services, or social skills classes. Encourage the development of an inclusive and empathetic school atmosphere.

9. Promote Self-Advocacy: Help your child learn how to advocate for themselves by assisting them in recognizing their abilities, obstacles, and the accommodations that facilitate their education. Encourage children to share their requirements and preferences with the faculty and staff at the school.

10. Extracurricular Activities: Look into extracurricular pursuits that complement your child's aptitudes and areas of interest. Engagement in sports, arts, or clubs can offer prospects for skill enhancement, interpersonal communication, and a feeling of achievement.

11. Attend Workshops and Support Groups: If you are a parent of a child with ADHD, you might want to think about going to workshops or support groups. These tools can offer insightful information, helpful tactics, and a network of other parents who are going through comparable difficulties.

Working together, advocating for your child, and having patience are all necessary when collaborating with schools to support your child with ADHD. You may contribute to the creation of an atmosphere that supports your child's academic and social success by encouraging open communication, training school personnel, and adjusting support to your child's specific requirements. Your advocacy and active participation can have a big impact on your child's educational path.

Individualized Education Plans (IEPs) for Children with ADHD

In order to give students with disabilities a customized framework for receiving the right educational assistance, the United States has made Individualized Education Plans (IEPs) legally required. An Individualized Education Plan (IEP) can be a useful tool for educators who want to customize their educational experience for kids with attention deficit hyperactivity disorder (ADHD). An examination of IEPs for kids with ADHD is provided below:

1. Understanding ADHD and Its Impact: It's essential to comprehend the nature of ADHD and how it impacts a kid's social and academic functioning in order to develop a successful IEP for a child with the disorder. This knowledge serves as the cornerstone for creating suitable objectives and modifications.

2. Eligibility and Evaluation: To find out if the kid is eligible for an IEP, an evaluation is conducted at the start of the procedure. In order to determine the child's needs, the evaluation usually entails assessments by educators and specialists. It is not necessary to have an ADHD diagnosis in order to be eligible.

3. Creating Measurable Objectives: The objectives in the child's IEP must be clear, quantifiable, and adapted to their particular needs and abilities. Objectives could focus on things like focus, planning, self-control, and academic achievement.

4. Accommodations and adjustments: The child's learning will be supported by the accommodations and adjustments outlined in the IEP. Extended time for homework and exams, first choice in seating, the use of assistive technology, and the availability of a quiet place to focus are a few examples.

5. Behavioral Supports: IEPs may contain tactics for handling ADHD-related behavioral issues. The application of behavior planning, social skills instruction, and positive reinforcement methods may be part of this.

6. Parent and Guardian Involvement: Throughout the creation and execution of the IEP, parents and guardians are essential. Their advocacy, worries, and comments are crucial in making sure the plan fits the child's objectives and requirements.

7. Consistent Reviews and Updates: IEPs are dynamic records. Periodic reviews and changes are applicable. These evaluations offer a chance to evaluate the child's development, modify objectives and adjustments as necessary, and make sure the IEP is still applicable.

8. Collaboration with School professionals: For the IEP to be implemented successfully, cooperation between teachers, special education professionals, and other school workers is essential. When there is effective communication, there is mutual understanding of the child's needs and the help being given.

9. Self-Advocacy and kid Involvement: As the kid becomes older, it's critical to support their growth in these areas as well as their participation in the IEP process. It is possible to help children with ADHD communicate their choices, identify their requirements, and participate fully in their schooling.

10. Transition Planning: To help older children get ready for life after school, transition planning may be included in their IEP. This could entail looking at higher education, vocational training, and employment options.

11. Legal Protections: The services and accommodations that a child with ADHD is entitled to receive are outlined in the legally enforceable Individualized Education Plan (IEP). It offers a foundation for the child's educational rights and is safeguarded under the Individuals with Disabilities Education Act (IDEA).

When it comes to making sure that kids with ADHD have access to the help and adjustments they require to thrive in a learning environment, an IEP is a useful tool. It acknowledges each child's distinct abilities and difficulties and offers a customized road map for their educational path. An IEP can be a useful tool in assisting students with ADHD to succeed in school via cooperation, advocacy, and frequent review.

Effective Homework and Study Strategies for Children with ADHD

Children with Attention Deficit Hyperactivity Disorder (ADHD) may find it especially difficult to focus, stay organized, and manage their time when doing homework and studying. Nonetheless, children with ADHD can excel academically and form productive study habits with the correct techniques and assistance. The following are some helpful study and homework tips for kids with ADHD:

1. Establish a Consistent Routine: Set up a regular study schedule that includes a quiet, well-organized room for schoolwork and a specified time. Children with ADHD benefit from consistency in knowing when to focus and what to expect.

2. Divide Up the Work into Doable Pieces: Big projects can be intimidating. Assist your youngster in breaking down assignments into smaller, more doable steps. To monitor progress, make use of checklists or a visual schedule.

3. Prioritize Tasks: Help your child learn how to order assignments according to their significance and due dates. They can avoid procrastinating by doing this and stay focused on what has to get done first.

4. Use a Timer: Set a timer for a short, concentrated amount of time, like 20 to 30 minutes, to work on a particular job. In between, take quick pauses to refuel. The Pomodoro method is a strategy that can increase productivity and focus.

5. Eliminate Distractions: Reduce them to a minimum in the study area. Make a quiet area, turn off electronics,

and close any tabs on the computer that aren't necessary. It could be advantageous for certain kids to wear noise-canceling headphones.

6. Arrange Materials: Show your kids how to arrange their materials. Make use of color-coding schemes, binders, and folders to make it easier for students to find tasks and materials.

7. Make Use of Visual Supports: Graphic organizers, charts, and diagrams are examples of visual aides that can assist kids with ADHD comprehend and retain information. Tasks and assignments have a clear framework thanks to visual aids.

8. Include Movement Breaks: Brief, active pauses are beneficial for kids with ADHD. To relieve extra energy, let them stretch, move around, or do brief physical activities.

9. Positive Reinforcement: Give yourself praise when you finish projects and remain on course. Your child may be inspired to stay focused and finish their work by receiving praise and rewards.

10. Promote Self-Advocacy: Instruct your kids to let their teachers know what they need. In the event that they need further help or clarification on an assignment, encourage them to ask for it.

11. Homework Buddy: You might want to think about assigning your child a study partner or "homework buddy". Peer support might provide them a chance for social engagement and help them stay on course.

12. Review and Preview: Before beginning homework, have your child go over the information from class and have a look at the lessons for the following day. Both readiness and retention may increase as a result.

13. Homework Planner: To assist your child in remembering assignments, deadlines, and exam dates, use a homework planner or app. Using a planner on a regular basis helps foster improved time management abilities.

14. Ask for Teacher Support: Keep in touch with the educators of your kids. Talk about the tactics that your child finds most effective, such as giving them more time to complete their homework or creating a quiet area in the classroom.

15. Take Professional Assistance Into Account: Should your child still have trouble with schoolwork and studying, think about getting help from an educational therapist or tutor who specializes in ADHD. Expert assistance might offer further tactics and direction.

Keep in mind that every child with ADHD is different, so figuring out the best study and homework techniques may require some trial and error. As your child strives for academic success, be patient with them, provide constant support, and acknowledge their efforts and successes.

Advocating for Your Child with ADHD

One of the most important roles parents and caregivers play in making sure their kid with Attention Deficit Hyperactivity Disorder (ADHD) get the support they need at school and in the community is advocating for them. The availability of suitable resources and assistance for your child can be greatly impacted by effective lobbying. The following are some essential ideas and tactics to help you speak up for your ADHD child:

1. Become knowledgeable about ADHD: Learn about the signs and symptoms, available treatments, and how it affects behavior and learning. When speaking out for your child, information is a really useful weapon.

2. Create a Support System: Get in touch with other parents, ADHD-related organizations, and support groups. These resources can offer insightful knowledge, consolation, and advocacy techniques.

3. Work Together with the School: Create a positive, open line of communication with your child's educators.

Communicate openly and honestly about your child's diagnosis, strengths, and difficulties.

4. Create an IEP or 504 Plan: To make sure your child gets the help and modifications they need in the classroom, collaborate with the school to create an Individualized Education Plan (IEP) or a 504 Plan.

5. Understand Your Child's Rights: Become knowledgeable on the rights and legal safeguards that apply to children with disabilities, such as those provided by Section 504 of the Rehabilitation Act and the Individuals with Disabilities Education Act (IDEA). Recognize the rights your child has and be ready to stand up for them.

6. Effective Communication: State your child's needs, objectives, and worries in plain language. Give particular instances of how ADHD affects your child's social and academic life. To create a cooperative relationship with teachers and other school personnel, use good communication.

7. Attend Meetings: Take part in parent-teacher conferences and IEP meetings, among other meetings pertaining to your child's education. Participate actively and empathetically, raising concerns and speaking up for your child's needs.

8. Document Everything: Maintain a file of all correspondence, meetings, and papers pertaining to the

education and ADHD of your child. When proving that support and accommodations are required, documentation can be quite helpful.

9. Seek Professional Advice: Talk to medical specialists, such as pediatricians, psychologists, or educational therapists, who specialize in ADHD. They can offer professional advice and evaluations to help with your advocacy work.

10. Put Your Attention on Solutions: When problems emerge, collaborate with school personnel to identify answers. Avoid placing blame on problems by approaching them with a problem-solving perspective. Finding appropriate answers to problems is frequently more successful when done together.

11. Keep Up to Date and Informed:
Keep up with changes in the science, medicine, and pedagogy around ADHD. As your child's requirements vary, advocacy activities might also need to adapt.

12. Promote Self-Advocacy: Inform your kids about their ADHD and the effects it has on them. As they get older, help them learn how to advocate for themselves by helping them express their wants and preferences to peers and teachers.

13. Be Tenacious: Promoting causes might take a lot of time. Don't let obstacles or failures demotivate you.

Remain steadfast in your determination to see to it that your child's requirements are fulfilled.

14. Collaborate with Medical Experts: Maintain in contact with medical experts who may offer advice on medication, counseling, and other facets of managing ADHD.

15. Access Community Resources: Look into regional and national resources, such as mental health associations, support groups for people with ADHD, and community services that offer aid and advocacy.

Being an advocate for your child with ADHD means having perseverance, tenacity, and a deep commitment to their welfare. Being aware of your child's particular requirements, working with teachers to meet those needs, being knowledgeable, and getting professional aid can all help you be a strong advocate for your child and foster an atmosphere where they can grow and realize their full potential.

CHAPTER 5: Coping with Emotional and Behavioral Challenges

Managing Impulsivity in Children with ADHD

One of the main signs of Attention Deficit Hyperactivity Disorder (ADHD) in kids is impulsivity. It may show itself as making snap decisions, finding it difficult to wait one's turn, or acting without thinking through the repercussions. For children with ADHD to make better decisions, have better social relationships, and achieve academic success, they must learn how to control their impulsivity. The following methods and approaches can help kids with ADHD control their impulsivity:

1. Executive Functioning Skills: Children with ADHD frequently have poor executive functioning skills, such as organizing, planning, and controlling impulsive behavior. It's critical to concentrate on improving these executive functions in order to assist them in managing impulsivity.

2. Cognitive Behavioral Therapy (CBT): This therapeutic method assists kids in identifying impulsive ideas and actions. It helps people to recognize their triggers,

assess the effects of their choices, and formulate plans to control when they react.

3. Self-Monitoring: Help kids with ADHD learn how to keep an eye on their own ideas and actions. Encourage children to pause, ponder the consequences of their actions, and then act on their instincts.

4. Pause and Breathe: Encourage people to employ the "pause and breathe" method. Encourage them to take a deep breath, count to five, and then respond when they feel an impulse. This brief stop can give them a chance to think twice before acting.

5. Mindfulness and Meditation: Children can learn self-awareness and self-control through mindfulness activities and meditation. Through these exercises, they can learn to notice their emotions and thoughts without jumping to conclusions.

6. Visual aids, such as posters or cues, can function as helpful reminders to pause and consider your actions before taking them. It can assist to place these in strategic areas like the child's bedroom or workspace.

7. Role-Playing: Play out scenarios in role-playing that frequently result in impulsive reactions. Practice thinking, alternative responses with your youngster.

8. Social Skills Training: Social interactions may be impacted by impulsivity. Enroll your child in social skills

groups or programs that emphasize acceptable social behavior, effective communication, and impulse control.

9. Promote Delayed Gratification: Teach your kids what delayed gratification is all about. Show them that sometimes it's better to wait for a reward or result rather than acting on impulse.

10. Establish Routines: Make predictable, well-organized daily routines. Anxiety and impulsive behavior might be lessened by knowing what to anticipate.

11. Apply Positive Reinforcement: Give your kids praise when they exhibit self-discipline and impulse control. Giving them praise can encourage them to keep up the good work.

12. Create Clearly Defined Boundaries: Set uniform, unambiguous guidelines and penalties for rash actions. Establish limits in a just and forceful manner.

13. Break Down Tasks: Assist your youngster in dividing assignments or tasks into more manageable chunks. This helps stop feeling overburdened and avoiding responsibilities on the spur of the moment.

14. medicine: A doctor's prescription medicine may be able to lessen impulsivity in some situations. If required, get advice from a psychiatrist or doctor to discuss your alternatives for medication.

15. Supportive Environment: Create an atmosphere that promotes candid dialogue. Assure your youngster that they can confide in you about their difficulties and impetuous behavior without worrying about facing consequences.

16. Set an example for others by acting with restraint and making deliberate decisions. Youngsters pick up lessons from the actions of reliable adults.

17. Empathy and Patience: Show your youngster empathy and patience as they work through their impulsive issues. Show them compassion and encouragement while they strive to develop better self-control.

For kids with ADHD, controlling impulsivity is a continuous effort that calls for perseverance and consistency. Children with ADHD can improve their interactions with others, make more deliberate decisions, and strengthen their impulse control by adopting these tactics and approaches into their everyday lives. Their success depends on a nurturing and caring atmosphere, so stay in constant contact with them and offer encouragement as they learn to control their impulsivity.

Dealing with Frustration and Anger

Due to issues with impulse control and emotional regulation, children diagnosed with Attention Deficit Hyperactivity Disorder (ADHD) sometimes have difficulty controlling their impatience and rage. It is vital to their wellbeing to teach them useful coping mechanisms for these feelings. The following methods and strategies can assist kids with ADHD in managing their annoyance and rage:

1. Identify Early Signs: Assist your child in recognizing the early mental and physical indicators of annoyance or rage. This could be characterized by tense muscles, fast breathing, or a tightness in the chest. Instruct them to heed these indications.

2. Deep Breathing: Instruct your kids in deep breathing techniques to help them relax when they become agitated or upset. It might be as easy as breathing deeply from your nose and out gently through your mouth.

3. Teach Your youngster to Count to Ten: Teach your youngster to wait ten seconds before retaliating in an annoying circumstance. This little delay can help them calm down and gather their thoughts before reacting rashly.

4. Encourage Your youngster to Use Positive Self-Talk: Help your youngster replace negative self-talk with positive affirmations. They can say, "I'll try my best," rather than, "I can't do this."

5. Visualize Calmness: When your child begins to get frustrated, help them to picture a serene and quiet environment. They can unwind and take their attention off of their rage by using this mental image.

6. Problem-Solving Techniques: Instruct your kids on problem-solving methods. Assist them in dissecting the frustrating problem into manageable components and investigate potential fixes.

7. Physical Activity: When your child is upset, get them moving by taking them for a stroll, a jog, or a trampoline jump. Exercise helps relax tension and lessen annoyance.

8. Art and Creativity: Help your child use art, such as journaling, painting, or sketching, as a means of expressing their feelings. These pursuits may be a constructive means of processing and letting go of annoyance.

9. Exercise Patience: Set an example and emphasize the value of patience. Remind your youngster that they may learn from their mistakes and that it's acceptable to have setbacks.

10. Time-Outs: Provide your kids a special area where they may retreat to when they're feeling overstimulated. They should be able to relax and restore control in this peaceful, safe setting.

11. Mindfulness and Meditation: Instruct your kids in mindfulness practices and meditation drills so they can maintain their composure in the face of frustration. They can maintain their composure and emotional control using mindfulness.

12. Validate Feelings: Explain to your kids that it's okay for them to feel angry and frustrated. It's critical that they feel heard and comprehended. Express empathy and validation.

13. Social Skills Training: To help your child better express themselves and control their emotions in social situations, think about enrolling them in social skills training courses.

14. Seek Professional Help: Speak with a mental health professional or therapist who specializes in ADHD and anger management if your child's irritation and anger become overpowering and negatively impact their everyday life.

15. Consistent Routine: Create a predictable and structured daily schedule. Anxiety and frustration might be lessened by knowing what to anticipate.

16. Positive Reinforcement: When your child successfully controls their irritation and anger, give them praise and rewards. They may be encouraged to keep applying these tactics if they receive positive reward.

17. Setting an Example: Take the lead by exhibiting constructive coping mechanisms for your own annoyance and fury. Youngsters pick up lessons from the actions of reliable adults.

One of the most important things in helping kids with ADHD learn how to regulate their emotions is teaching them how to deal with frustration and rage. You can help your child better manage these difficult emotions and get by in everyday life by following these strategies and creating a nurturing and understanding atmosphere. As your child works on controlling their irritation and anger, keep in mind that development could be slow. Be patient and provide constant support.

Building Self-Esteem

Children who suffer from Attention Deficit Hyperactivity Disorder (ADHD) may encounter distinct obstacles that could potentially affect their self-worth. Academic performance, impulsivity, and attention issues can all lead to low self-esteem. Children with ADHD need to have a strong sense of self-worth in order to flourish.

The following techniques can help them feel more confident:

1. Promote Self-Awareness: Assist your child in comprehending the meaning of their ADHD diagnosis. Since self-awareness is the first step towards developing self-esteem, encourage them to acknowledge their strengths and weaknesses.

2. Have Reasonably High Expectations: Try not to have too high expectations for your child. Acknowledge each person's unique talents and assist them in concentrating on realistic objectives. No matter how insignificant they may seem, acknowledge their accomplishments.

3. Praise Effort, Not Just Results: Commend your youngster for their diligence and tenacity rather than concentrating just on the outcome. Stress the value of giving it your all and taking lessons from mistakes.

4. Create achievement Opportunities: Set up circumstances in which your kids can achieve achievement. Promote engagement in pursuits that they find enjoyable and fulfilling, be it athletics, the arts, or hobbies. Conviction produces assurance.

5. Teach Coping Skills: Assist your child in learning coping skills to control their ADHD symptoms. As kids become more independent, teaching them time management, organization, and impulse control skills can help them feel better about themselves.

6. Encourage Self-Advocacy: Help your child communicate their needs, preferences, and difficulties to classmates and instructors. Self-advocacy gives individuals the confidence to ask for help and modifications when needed.

7. Highlight Your Child's Strengths: Acknowledge and value your child's abilities. Showcasing their strengths might help them feel more confident and good about themselves.

8. Refrain from Labeling: Steer clear of assigning your child derogatory labels associated with their ADHD. Pay attention to their strengths and abilities rather than their weaknesses.

9. Encourage a Growth Mindset: Explain to your kids the idea of a growth mindset and stress that skills and intellect can be acquired by work and education. This kind of thinking promotes self-worth and resiliency.

10. Promote Social Connections: Assist your child in forming wholesome bonds with classmates who value and encourage them. A sense of belonging and self-worth can be provided by social interactions.

11. Show Unconditional Love: No matter what obstacles they face, make sure your child knows they are loved and accepted for who they are. A positive self-esteem is fostered by unconditional affection.

12. Encourage Self-Care: Instruct your kids on the value of self-care, which includes a healthy diet, regular exercise, and enough sleep. A positive self-image is correlated with physical well-being.

13. Celebrate Progress: Give your child credit for any advancements they make in controlling their ADHD. Every advancement is a noteworthy accomplishment.

14. Professional Support: You should think about consulting a therapist or counselor who specializes in working with children with ADHD if your child's self-esteem is severely affected.

15. Set an Example: Show compassion and respect for yourself in your own life. Your example will teach your youngster.

16. Promote Perseverance: Show your kids that life is full with obstacles and disappointments. Motivate them to keep going and take lessons from their mistakes.

For kids with ADHD, fostering self-worth is a continuous struggle. Be kind and gentle with your child as they strive for increased self-assurance. Supporting your child, highlighting their talents, and teaching them coping mechanisms will help them build the resilience and positive self-image they need to succeed in school and in life.

Addressing Anxiety and Depression

Children diagnosed with ADHD (attention deficit hyperactivity disorder) may be more susceptible to anxiety and depression. These emotional problems may be exacerbated by the difficulty patients encounter in coping with their symptoms and going about their daily lives. In order to promote their general well-being, anxiety and depression must be addressed. The following techniques can assist kids with ADHD in controlling their anxiety and depression:

1. Encourage your youngster to communicate about their experiences and feelings through open communication. Provide a secure, accepting environment for them to express their feelings.

2. Professional Assessment: Seek a mental health specialist for a professional assessment if you believe your child is suffering from anxiety or depression. An accurate diagnosis is necessary for successful treatment.

3. Therapeutic Support: To treat anxiety and depression, think about treatment, such as cognitive-behavioral therapy (CBT). CBT can assist kids in developing coping mechanisms and challenging harmful mental patterns.

4. Medication Evaluation: If your child's everyday life is being severely impacted by anxiety or depression, speak with a healthcare provider about your options for medication. In certain situations, medication may be advised.

5. Offer Reassurance: Let your youngster know that they are not alone and that their feelings of sadness and fear are not their fault. Inform them of your availability to assist them.

6. Establlsh a Routine: To offer stability and predictability, establish a defined daily routine. Anticipating things can lessen anxiety and symptoms of depression.

7. Promote physical activity: Studies have shown that regular exercise boosts mood and lessens depressive and anxious symptoms. Get your kids involved in enjoyable physical activities.

8. Eating Well: Eating a well-balanced diet has a good effect on mental health. Make sure your kids are eating wholesome meals that promote their wellbeing.

9. Sleep Hygiene: Develop sound sleeping practices because getting too little sleep can make depression and anxiety symptoms worse. Promote a regular sleep regimen.

10. Stress Reduction Methods: Instruct your kids in deep breathing, mindfulness, and meditation, among other relaxation and stress-reduction methods.

11. Social Support: Help your child to keep up relationships with friends and relatives who understand and are there for them emotionally.

12. Don't Overload: Take care not to give your kids too many extracurricular activities or duties. Make sure they have time to unwind and rest.

13. Monitor Screen Time: Avoid spending too much time on screens, especially right before bed. Anxiety and depression symptoms may worsen as a result of excessive screen use.

14. Encourage Your Child to Pursue Interests and Hobbies: Giving your child a sense of direction and fulfillment can come from supporting their interests and hobbies.

15. Set an Example: Showcase healthy coping mechanisms and self-care in your own life. Your example will teach your youngster.

16. Establish a Supportive Environment: Provide a loving, accepting, and supportive household for your child. Provide empathy and emotional support.

17. Have patience: Anxiety and depression management is a continuous effort. Regarding your child's development, exercise patience and give them constant support.

Teaching Coping Skills

Children with Attention Deficit Hyperactivity Disorder (ADHD) need to learn how to cope with life when they are faced with difficulties in controlling their symptoms. Children who learn these coping mechanisms may find it easier to control their impulsivity, impatience, and attention issues. The following techniques can be used to teach kids with ADHD coping skills:

1. Self-Awareness: Assist your child in realizing how their behavior and emotions are impacted by their ADHD symptoms. An important first step is to comprehend the relationship between their condition and their conduct.

2. Recognize Triggers: Assist your child in identifying typical sources of their difficulties, such as impatience, distraction, or impulsivity. They can predict and control their responses if they are aware of what causes their symptoms.

3. Emotional Recognition: Help your child learn to identify their feelings, such as rage, frustration, enthusiasm, and anxiety. The first step in learning coping mechanisms is for individuals to comprehend their feelings.

4. Deep Breathing: Instruct your child in deep breathing techniques to assist them relax when they're feeling stressed. Stress and anxiety can be reduced by taking deep breaths through the nose and gently releasing them through the mouth.

5. Mindfulness and Meditation: To assist your child in being grounded and in the present moment, teach them mindfulness and meditation skills. These exercises can help them become more in control of their emotions and self.

6. Positive Self-Talk: Teach your youngster to use positive self-talk to counteract any negative thoughts. As an alternative to statins, "I can't do this," they could add, "I can try my best."

7. Visualizations: Help your child visualize a serene and tranquil environment. They can refocus their attention and unwind with the aid of this visualization.

8. Problem-Solving Skills: To help your child deal with issues related to their ADHD, teach them problem-solving strategies. Assist them in decomposing

issues into smaller, more manageable components and investigate possible fixes.

9. Time Management: Give your kids the resources and techniques they need to manage their time more effectively. This might lessen the tension and annoyance that come with being hurried or unorganized.

10. Stress Reduction Techniques: Teach your child how to tense and release different muscle groups in order to relieve physical tension. One such technique is progressive muscle relaxation.

11. Promote Physical Activity: Engaging in regular physical activity helps enhance focus and lower stress levels. Get your kids involved in sports, dance, yoga, or other activities they find enjoyable.

12. Creative Outlets: Encourage your kids to use art mediums like journaling, painting, or sketching to communicate their emotions. Expressing oneself creatively can be healing.

13. Role-Playing: Take part in role-playing exercises that imitate actual events that cause emotional responses. With your youngster, practice other, more positive reactions.

14. Social Skills Training: Take into account signing up your kids for classes or programs that teach social skills.

Better social skills can help them better control their emotions in social situations.

15. Promote Flexibility: Instill in your kids the value of flexibility and adaptability in order to deal with unforeseen changes or interruptions to their daily schedule.

16. Set an Example: Use healthy coping mechanisms in your own life. Youngsters pick up lessons from the actions of reliable adults.

17. Exercise Patience: Show patience while your child picks up and uses coping mechanisms. They may make slow progress, so you will need to provide them constant encouragement and support.

By imparting coping skills, you enable your child to overcome the difficulties brought on by ADHD and go through everyday life with more resilience and self-assurance. These abilities can eventually enhance their general well-being by assisting them in managing impulsivity, frustration, and concentration issues more skillfully.

CHAPTER 6: Social Skills and Friendships

Developing Social Awareness

Due to issues with impulse control, attention span, and emotional regulation, children diagnosed with Attention Deficit Hyperactivity Disorder (ADHD) may find it challenging to function in social situations. To successfully navigate social encounters and forge meaningful relationships, it is imperative that they develop social awareness. The following techniques can help kids with ADHD increase their social awareness:

1. Self-Awareness: Start by assisting your child in recognizing their own advantages and disadvantages in relation to ADHD. The basis of social awareness is self-awareness.

2. Instruct Emotion Recognition: Assist your child in identifying and comprehending various emotions in both themselves and others. To model emotional expressions, use role-playing, movies, or books.

3. Encourage your child to practice perspective-taking by showing them how to view things from the viewpoint of others. Talk about other people's perspectives in

various situations to foster compassion and comprehension.

4. Recognize Social Cues: Help your youngster learn to interpret nonverbal clues like tone of voice, body language, and facial expressions. Comprehending the emotions and intentions of others requires a comprehension of these cues.

5. Role-Playing: Take part in role-playing games that imitate authentic social settings. Practice reacting appropriately to various social cues and situations.

6. Instruct Active Listening: Stress the value of attentive listening. To demonstrate that they are paying attention to the conversation, encourage your child to keep eye contact, nod, and pose questions.

7. Social Stories: Read or tell stories that highlight particular social circumstances and how to respond to them. Children can learn and retain social expectations from these stories.

8. Group Activities: Promote your child's involvement in clubs and group activities where they can socialize with classmates in a controlled setting. Social skills can be practiced through group activities.

9. Friendship Skills Training: You might want to think about signing up your kids for classes that teach them how to make and keep friends.

10. Watch Your Emotions: Teach your kids to identify when they're feeling stressed or overwhelmed in social settings. Urge them to use self-calming strategies or take breaks.

11. Social Skills Groups: Enroll your kids in or start your own social skills groups so they can practice making friends and learn from one another in a safe setting.

12. Establish Social Goals: Assist your child in establishing clear social objectives, including striking up a discussion with a classmate or maintaining eye contact when speaking. Honor their accomplishments.

13. Set an Example for Social Behavior: Act appropriately in social situations and when interacting with your child. Youngsters frequently pick up social skills from watching adults.

14. Promote Open Communication: Give your kids a safe, accepting environment in which they can talk about their social experiences, difficulties, and emotions. Be a sympathetic ear.

15. Have Patience: Recognize that becoming socially conscious takes time. As your child works to develop their social skills, have patience with them and provide constant support.

16. Deal with Peer Pressure and Bullying: Talk to your kids about peer pressure and bullying. Assist them in identifying these circumstances and knowing how to react with confidence and assertiveness.

For kids with ADHD, gaining social awareness is a continuous process. You may enable your child to navigate social situations, understand others, and form meaningful relationships by giving them advice, practicing social skills, and creating chances for social interactions. Their general well-being and achievement in social and academic contexts can both be greatly enhanced by social awareness.

Building Friendships

A child's social and emotional development greatly benefits from friendships, but children with Attention Deficit Hyperactivity Disorder (ADHD) may experience particular difficulties making and keeping friends. The following techniques can assist kids with ADHD in making wholesome friendships:

1. Social Skills Training: Enroll your child in classes that teach social skills, with an emphasis on friendship-building, communicating, and interpreting social cues. These courses can offer useful tactics.

2. Teach Conversation Skills: Assist your child in honing conversational skills like eye contact, attentive listening, and speaking in turns, you can help them practice these.

3. Role-playing: Play role-playing games with your kids to mimic everyday social situations. They can pick up on how to strike up discussions and interact with people by doing this.

4. Promote Common Interests: Assist your youngster in discovering and pursuing passion projects and hobbies. Getting involved in clubs or groups that share these hobbies can help you naturally connect with other people who share your interests.

5. Schedule Playdates: Make plans for playdates or excursions with neighbors or classmates. Your youngster can form closer bonds in these one-on-one or small group situations.

6. Encourage Your Child to Join Clubs and Activities: Get your kids involved in clubs that suit their interests, sports teams, or extracurricular activities. Friendships can be cultivated by shared interests.

7. Teach Conflict Resolution: Instruct your kids on how to settle disputes amicably. They ought to be aware of the significance of offering an apology, extending forgiveness, and resolving conflicts.

8. Befriend Your Child: Take on the role of a "friend coach" for them. Talk about the characteristics of a good friend, such as reliability, kindness, and empathy.

9. Set a good example for friendship: Act out good friendship behaviors in your own interactions. Youngsters learn up knowledge by watching grownups.

10. Foster Empathy: Foster empathy by talking about the thoughts, emotions, and experiences of others. Urge your youngster to think about the impact of their actions on other people.

11. Establish a Supportive Environment: Provide a loving and accepting household for your youngster. Promote candid discussion on their social experiences.

12. Have Patience and Understanding: Recognize that forming friendships can be difficult. While your child develops their social skills, have patience and offer them emotional support.

13. Deal with Bullying and Peer Pressure: Inform your child about bullying and peer pressure, and assist them in creating assertive and self-assured coping mechanisms.

14. Monitor Screen Time: Avoid spending too much time in front of a screen as this can impede the chance to make in-person friendships.

15. Seek Support: Get in touch with educators, school counselors, and support organizations that focus on social skills and ADHD. They can offer insightful advice.

16. Promote Independence: Motivate your kids to take the lead in social circumstances. Even if you can help, it's crucial that they form their own friendships.

Although it could take some time, children with ADHD can create deep relationships with their classmates via social skill development and your assistance. Encouragement, opportunities for socialization, and direction are all important while your child attempts to form healthy connections.

Handling Bullying and Peer Pressure

Due to their particular difficulties in social situations, children with Attention Deficit Hyperactivity Disorder (ADHD) may be especially susceptible to bullying and peer pressure. It's crucial to give them the abilities and information needed to deal with these circumstances. The following techniques can assist kids with ADHD in overcoming peer pressure and bullying:

1. Encourage Open Communication: Talk to your child in an honest and nonjudgmental manner. Urge them to discuss their social experiences, especially any

instances of bullying or peer pressure they may have come across.

2. Encourage Assertiveness: Show your kids how to boldly and calmly make their own decisions. Students can practice forceful responses to peer pressure by role-playing various scenarios.

3. Help Your Child Recognize Bullying: Teach your child to identify the telltale signs of bullying, which can include exclusion, verbal or physical assault, and cyberbullying. Urge children to tell an adult they can trust about any instances.

4. Create an Action Plan: Work with your child to come up with a strategy for handling bullying. This method may involve talking to a teacher, asking a counselor for assistance, or consulting a parent.

5. Promote Self-Esteem: Assist your youngster in developing confidence and self-worth. Bullying and peer pressure are less likely to have an impact on kids who are confident in themselves.

6. Establish Boundaries: Help your child understand the value of establishing personal boundaries and the necessity of saying "no" to requests or circumstances that make them uncomfortable.

7. Talk About Peer Pressure: Hold candid conversations regarding peer pressure and any possible

repercussions. Describe how it's acceptable to defy peer pressure and make decisions on your own.

8. Role-playing: Give your kids practice reacting to peer pressure by having them act out scenarios. Give advice on how to say "no" without being afraid.

9. Teach Problem-Solving: Assist your youngster in acquiring the ability to solve problems. Urge them to consider carefully the possible effects of their choices and behaviors.

10. Keep an Eye on Online Activity: Talk to your kids about safe internet use and keep an eye on their online activities. Instruct students on the need of maintaining one's privacy when sharing personal information online.

11. Seek Support: Talk to teachers, school counselors, or other experts who can offer advice and action if bullying or peer pressure becomes a recurring problem.

12. Encourage Your youngster to Form Positive Friendships: Help your youngster form respectful, encouraging relationships with others. These connections may serve as a safety net.

13. Be a Source of help: Show your child that they may confide in you without worrying about being judged and that you are there to help them. Assure them that they can safely ask for assistance when necessary.

14. Encourage Resilience: Instill in your kids the capacity to overcome hardship and persevere in the face of difficulty. Assist them in realizing that difficult situations can teach them and help them grow.

15. Handle Self-Esteem Issues: To handle the emotional fallout, take your child into consideration for counseling or therapy if bullying or peer pressure has a detrimental effect on their sense of self.

Managing peer pressure and bullying calls for constant supervision, support, and communication. Giving your kids the tools they need to overcome these obstacles will enable them to become resilient and make wise decisions in trying circumstances.

Supporting Positive Relationships

Children with Attention Deficit Hyperactivity Disorder (ADHD) need to improve their social and emotional skills by establishing and sustaining meaningful interactions. The following techniques can aid in the growth of wholesome relationships:

1. Teach Your Child Effective Communication Skills: Assist your child in acquiring these abilities, which include interpreting non-verbal cues, active listening,

and clear expression. Urge them to be curious and ask questions of others.

2. Foster Empathy: Instruct your kids to appreciate and comprehend the thoughts and emotions of others. Talk about events from various perspectives and promote empathy as the cornerstone of wholesome interpersonal interactions.

3. Set an Example of Healthy Relationships: Show off your personal interactions with friends, family, and your child by acting in a courteous and cheerful manner. Youngsters frequently pick up relational skills from watching adults.

4. Promote Shared Interests: Help your kids discover their hobbies and areas of interest. Promote engagement in hobbies-related activities and facilitate connections amongst like-minded peers.

5. Promote Social Opportunities: Set up planned social activities, playdates, and group outings so your kids may socialize with their peers. These environments offer chances for social growth.

6. Teach Conflict Resolution: Assist your youngster in learning how to settle disputes amicably. Urge them to express regret, extend forgiveness, and work out their differences.

7. Establish Boundaries: Instruct your kids to respect others' boundaries as well as their own. This aids in laying a respectful basis for their interactions.

8. Be a Source of Support: Assure your child that you are here to help them form and sustain healthy relationships. Be a sympathetic ear and provide assistance when required.

9. Handle Social Challenges: Take the initiative to help your child with any social issues they may encounter. Develop successful techniques in collaboration with educators, school counselors, and specialists who specialize in ADHD.

10. Promote Inclusion: Teach your kids to be inclusive and to include others. Reach out to classmates who might require a friend in order to foster a feeling of community.

Encourage your youngster to take the lead in social situations to foster independence. Even though you should be there to guide them, they should also have the chance to form relationships on their own.

12. Talk About Digital Etiquette: Instruct your kids in appropriate online conduct and digital manners. Talk about how important it is to behave with kindness and respect when interacting online.

13. Celebrate Friendship: Give your kids a chance to enjoy and cultivate their friendships. Recognize the importance of having healthy relationships in their lives.

14. Dealing with Peer Pressure: Have a conversation with your kids about peer pressure and how it could affect their relationships. Show children how to stand up for themselves and make decisions on their own.

15. Set an Example for Problem-Solving: Show off your ability to solve problems in your personal interactions. This can teach your youngster how to resolve conflicts and obstacles in a positive way.

16. Have patience: Recognize that establishing and preserving healthy relationships takes time. As your child works on social development, have patience with them and provide constant encouragement.

You may support and guide your child with ADHD in forming and sustaining healthy relationships that enhance their social and emotional development by putting these techniques into practice. Healthy relationships are critical to their development and success in a variety of spheres of life.

CHAPTER 7: ADHD in Adolescence

Puberty and Hormonal Changes

Significant hormonal, emotional, and physical changes occur during adolescence, and these changes may have particular effects on people with attention deficit hyperactivity disorder (ADHD). In order to effectively help students throughout this transitional age, parents, caregivers, and educators must have a thorough understanding of the interaction between ADHD and puberty. Here are some crucial things to remember:

1. Hormonal Changes: Puberty and other hormonal changes are brought on by adolescence. These modifications may have an impact on behavior, emotions, and mood. These changes in hormones may exacerbate impulsive and emotional dysregulation in people with ADHD.

2. Emotional Chaos: During puberty, adolescents with ADHD may encounter more intense emotional difficulties. Anxiety, impatience, and mood swings may become more noticeable. It's critical to understand that these emotional swings are a normal aspect of growing up.

3. prescription Modifications: Because of fluctuating hormone levels, some teenagers with ADHD may need to make modifications to their prescription schedules. To guarantee that ADHD drugs remain effective, speaking with a healthcare professional is crucial.

4. Academic Demands: Adolescence brings with it increasingly demanding academic requirements. It may get harder for teenagers with ADHD to maintain organization, time management, and focus over time. When necessary, parents and teachers should offer structure, support, and accommodations.

5. Impulsivity and Risk-Taking: Some teenagers with ADHD may exhibit greater impulsivity and risk-taking behavior as a result of hormonal changes. They might be more likely to act impulsively, which could lead to dangerous behaviors or drug experiments.

6. Self-Esteem: As they deal with the difficulties of puberty, adolescents with ADHD may see swings in their self-esteem. To increase their self-confidence, it's critical to offer them emotional support, recognize their accomplishments, and play to their talents.

7. Peer interactions: Because of their impulsivity and trouble reading social signs, adolescents with ADHD may experience particular difficulty in peer interactions. Encourage them to form healthy friendships and help them develop their social skills.

8. Emotional management: To assist teenagers manage the highs and lows of adolescence, teach them emotional management skills. Techniques like cognitive-behavioral therapy, deep breathing, and mindfulness can be beneficial.

9. Self-Advocacy: Help teenagers learn how to advocate for themselves. Assist them in expressing their wants and preferences to teachers and medical professionals, particularly if they require prescription modifications.

10. Routine and Consistency: Keep your home environment routine and consistent. Routines that limit stress and provide consistency can be beneficial for adolescents diagnosed with ADHD.

11. Open Communication: Provide a free-flowing, accepting environment where teenagers can talk about their struggles and experiences. Invite them to express their emotions and worries.

It is crucial to comprehend how puberty-related hormonal changes affect teenagers with ADHD in order to provide them with appropriate care and to ensure their wellbeing. Teenagers can traverse adolescence with better resilience and success if parents and educators address the particular obstacles that develop during this transitional era.

Transitioning to Middle and High School

For students with Attention Deficit Hyperactivity Disorder (ADHD), moving from elementary to middle and high school is a big turning point in their education. It can also present new opportunities as well as difficulties. As students with ADHD make this transition, parents, caregivers, and educators should keep the following in mind:

1. Greater Independence: Students have more freedom to arrange their timetables and responsibilities in middle and high schools. In order to manage the demands of greater academic work, adolescents with ADHD may require assistance in building strong executive functioning skills.

2. Academic Rigor: Middle and high school students face more challenging academic requirements. To thrive academically, students with ADHD may need assistance in areas like time management, organization, and study techniques.

3. Medication Management: During this change, it's critical to make sure the student's ADHD medication continues to work. Speak with medical professionals about when and how to administer medication, as well as any required modifications.

4. Advocate for Accommodations: In the educational system, parents and other caregivers should speak up for the essential accommodations. Extended time for assignments or tests, access to study resources, and preferred seats are a few examples of these allowances.

5. Open Communication: To address any issues or problems that may come up, keep lines of communication open with educators, counselors, and school administration. Frequent check-ins can assist in quickly identifying and resolving problems.

6. Self-Advocacy Skills: Motivate pupils to hone their advocacy abilities. Teach them how to express their preferences and needs to the staff members of the school; this will come in handy especially when they are in high school.

7. Social and Emotional Support: During this shift, adolescents with ADHD may experience particular social and emotional difficulties. Encourage the growth of their social skills and emotional control to aid in their peer relationship navigation.

8. Transition Planning: Develop a strategy for managing academic work, organization, and emotional well-being in collaboration with the school.

9. Consistent Routines: To reduce stress and anxiety related to the change, maintain consistent routines at home that offer structure and predictability.

10. Monitoring and Feedback: Keep an eye on the student's emotional health and academic development on a regular basis. Ask teachers and counselors for input to make sure the student is adjusting to the changes.

11. Promote Extracurricular Activities: Promote your students' involvement in organizations and extracurricular activities that suit their interests. These pursuits can bring one a feeling of purpose and community.

12. Academic Objectives: Work with the learner to establish reasonable objectives. Celebrate their accomplishments and thank them for their hard work.

For adolescents with ADHD, the move to middle and high school can be extremely difficult, but it can also present a chance for personal growth and development if the right help and direction are provided. A smooth transition to this new academic chapter can be ensured by parents, caregivers, and educators attending to the special requirements of these youngsters.

Preparing Adolescents with ADHD for the Future

The adolescent years are critical for helping people with Attention Deficit Hyperactivity Disorder (ADHD) get ready for adulthood. It's a time of change, introspection, and increasing independence. In order to assist teenagers with ADHD in laying a solid basis for their future, take into account the following tactics:

1. Self-Advocacy: Instruct teenagers on how to stand up for themselves in social and academic contexts. To help children become more self-aware and self-assured, encourage them to share their wants and preferences with teachers and peers.

2. Academic Planning: Create a thorough academic plan in collaboration with the school. In order to support the student's academic success, this plan should take into account their strengths, shortcomings, and accommodations.

3. Job Exploration: Start looking into possible job options and hobbies. To assist adolescents in making well-informed decisions about their future, take into account career counseling, internships, and aptitude testing.

4. Executive Functioning Skills: To provide teenagers the resources they need for academic achievement,

continue to support executive functioning skills including time management, organization, and study methods.

5. Medication Management: Continue to have frequent discussions with medical professionals to guarantee that medication is still effective and is changed as needed. Urge teenagers to assume accountability for managing their medications.

6. Emotional Regulation: Teach teenagers how to manage their emotions in order to help them deal with stress, anxiety, and emotional difficulties. Capabilities like relaxation and awareness can be quite helpful.

7. Social Skills Development: Encourage the growth of social skills such as interpreting social signs, resolving conflicts, and building peer connections. If required, take into account social skills training courses.

8. Goal-Setting: Work with teenagers to establish both immediate and long-term objectives. Honor their achievements and emphasize the value of perseverance in the face of difficulty.

9. Independent Living Skills: To make teenagers ready for independent living in the future, start teaching them basic life skills like time management, cooking, and budgeting.

10. College and Career Planning: Talk about career and college alternatives. Find institutions and colleges that

provide ADHD support services, and look into financial planning and scholarship alternatives.

11. Positive Reinforcement: Keep offering emotional support and positive reinforcement. Teens with ADHD may experience obstacles, and your support can be a great source of inspiration.

12. Future Vision: Help teenagers to clearly define their goals and envision their future selves. Assist them in realizing that, with enough effort and perseverance, they can accomplish their goals despite having ADHD.

13. Focus on Resilience: Instruct teenagers on the value of resilience and the capacity to overcome hardship. Assist them in developing a growth mentality.

14. Seek Professional Advice: You might want to speak with experts in the fields of teenage development and ADHD. Their knowledge can offer insightful advice and direction.

15. Encourage Independence: While assistance is necessary, progressively encourage individuality in making choices and addressing issues. Give teenagers more freedom to accept accountability for their decisions and actions.

The process of preparing teenagers with ADHD for the future is continuous and calls for tolerance, commitment, and teamwork. You may assist them in laying a solid basis for a prosperous and satisfying future by attending to their specific requirements and putting an emphasis on skill development.

CHAPTER 8: Parenting Strategies for Long-Term Success

Patience and Persistence

Two crucial traits for helping people with Attention Deficit Hyperactivity Disorder (ADHD) are perseverance and patience. Whether addressing ADHD in childhood or adulthood, the path is characterized by particular difficulties and achievements. Let's examine these attributes' significance in more detail:

Patience:

1. Understanding: Gaining patience starts with being aware of how ADHD works. The first step in developing empathy and patience is realizing that people with

ADHD frequently struggle with impulse control, inattention, and hyperactivity.

2. Learning Curve: Managing ADHD requires some learning. It's important to recognize that setbacks might happen and that progress might not always happen right away. It takes patience to withstand these changes.

3. Non-Judgmental Support: It's critical to offer non-judgmental support. Even though people with ADHD occasionally make errors or encounter difficulties, patience enables you to support and encourage them without passing judgment.

4. Emotional Regulation: Promote the growth of emotional control abilities. As people learn to properly control their emotions and reactions, patience will be needed.

5. Academic and Behavioral Development: Show patience as these areas develop. Although managing ADHD frequently involves failures, even little victories add up over time.

Persistence:

1. Consistency: Maintaining an ADHD treatment plan requires persistent efforts. Sustaining a schedule, framework, and therapy interventions can help lead to successful results.

2. Advocacy: It takes tenacious work to guarantee that people with ADHD receive the modifications and assistance they require in employment and educational environments.

3. Developing skills: Developing executive functioning and coping abilities requires patience and perseverance. Maintain your progress with organization, self-control, and time management.

4. Medication Management: Managing medications may need some trial and error. The key to determining the ideal drug and dosage is perseverance.

5. Life Skills: Instruct students in life skills like problem-solving, cooking, and budgeting. These abilities can need continuing practice and instruction.

6. Communication: Keep lines of communication open and continuous with those who have ADHD. It takes perseverance to establish a setting where they are at ease talking about their struggles and accomplishments.

7. Resilience: Foster resilience by continually highlighting the fact that obstacles are a necessary part of the path. ADHD sufferers are able to grow and learn from their experiences.

8. Future Planning: Keep encouraging goal-setting and future planning. In order to lead people toward their long-term goals, persistence is crucial.

The keys to managing ADHD effectively are perseverance and patience. They establish a nurturing atmosphere that enables people to grow, learn, and prosper in spite of whatever obstacles they may encounter. By continuously exhibiting these attributes, you can assist those with ADHD in developing the abilities and self-assurance they require to lead happy, full lives.

Self-Care for Parents of Children with ADHD

It can be a fulfilling but challenging job to care for a child with attention deficit hyperactivity disorder (ADHD). Prioritizing self-care is essential for parents who want to help their child properly and preserve their own wellbeing. The following are self-care techniques:

1. Seek Support: Make connections with specialists who are aware of the difficulties associated with ADHD, other parents, and support organizations. Offering guidance and experiences to others can be a great way to get assistance.

2. Set Boundaries: To strike a balance between your own time and your caregiving responsibilities, set

boundaries. Make sure your family members understand what you need and ask for help.

3. Professional Guidance: To help manage stress, emotional difficulties, and the effects of caregiving, think about attending therapy or counseling sessions. A mental health specialist is able to offer coping mechanisms.

4. Physical Health: Give your body the attention it deserves by getting enough sleep, eating a balanced diet, and exercising frequently. A healthy body has more resilience to stress and has more energy to give care.

5. Take Breaks: Give yourself frequent pauses, even if they are only brief. These little breaks can assist you in refocusing and recharging.

6. Hobbies and Interests: Continue to pursue your interests and hobbies. Taking part in the things you enjoy might offer a much-needed break from everyday obligations.

7. Establish a Connection with Your Partner: If appropriate, cultivate your partnership. You and your partner can overcome the difficulties of raising an ADHD child by being open with each other and working together.

8. Time Management: Use time-management strategies and prioritize tasks to effectively manage your time. You

can spend more time alone and feel less stressed as a result.

9. Self-Reflection: Examine yourself to learn about your needs and feelings. Recognize burnout symptoms and take appropriate action.

10. Be Kind to Yourself: Keep in mind that it's acceptable to have restrictions and periods of annoyance. Recognize your efforts as a parent and treat yourself with compassion.

11. Assign Responsibilities: Assign caregiving duties to other family members or, if required, think about obtaining professional assistance.

12. Establish a Supportive Environment: Make your home a compassionate and understanding place. Promote collaboration and honest communication within the family.

13. Make Long-Term Plans: Think about long-term strategies for your child's upbringing and future. This can lessen uncertainties and bring about peace of mind.

14. Honor Yourself and Your Child's Accomplishments: Honor your own and your child's accomplishments. Acknowledge your accomplishments and the role you have played in your child's development.

15. Respite Care: Look into solutions for short-term relief from a skilled caregiver. This protects your child's wellbeing and lets you take a break.

16. Remain Informed: Keep up your knowledge on ADHD. Gaining knowledge about the illness will improve your ability to support your child and handle stress.

17. Make relaxation a priority: To reduce stress and anxiety, make relaxation practices like deep breathing, meditation, or mindfulness a part of your everyday routine.

For parents of children with ADHD, self-care is not an option; it is a need. You can better support and love your child and lead a healthy, balanced life if you take care of your physical, emotional, and psychological well-being.

Celebrating Achievements

Celebrations of all kinds are taking place all around us: new jobs, weddings, reunions of friends and family after a separation of more than a year, graduations, you name it, and with good cause! Significant life events, achievements, and turning points are unquestionably worthy of celebration. Still, not everybody is having a party. Some folks are feeling uncertain or disappointed. They can't keep up with the expectations that life keeps hurling at them. They didn't get the grades they wanted or expected. They don't have a summer internship or job yet. They didn't get the promotion they had hoped for. They don't know where they will attend school in the fall.

These situations are all too familiar to those who suffer from ADHD, but they also yearn to celebrate and be recognized for their achievements, to live up to expectations both of others and of themselves, to make the Dean's list, to receive a promotion, and to fulfill their commitments. They don't live their lives hoping to let themselves down or let others down. In fact, we frequently hear from people asking themselves, "Why can't I just do it?" Unfortunately, professionals, teachers, and parents often interpret these behaviors or lack thereof as deliberate, willful, or motivated by a lack of desire, which only serves to reinforce the feelings of disappointment, guilt, and "brokenness" that the person with ADHD continues to experience. What if we saw the individual as lacking the necessary abilities, offered them support and empathy, and shared in their disappointment? We could also look for their small victories and rejoice with them, rather than viewing them as lazy or uninspired. There are many challenges, and they are easily visible since they occur frequently during the day, are noticed by others, and are frequently called out. It's time to recognize and celebrate the accomplishments of individuals with ADHD, no matter how big or tiny, as every day is worth celebrating and small victories can build up to big ones!

Conclusion

Navigating ADHD with Strength and Resilience

While managing Attention Deficit Hyperactivity Disorder (ADHD) is a difficult and sometimes difficult path, it is also one that is characterized by hope, resiliency, and strength. People with ADHD, along with their families and support systems, have particular difficulties from the time of their diagnosis through the changes that come with growing up, becoming an adult, and transitioning into children. This thorough ADHD parenting guide for boys has helped with this journey by offering advice, tactics, and support.

ADHD is not a handicap; rather, it is a characteristic of the person with ADHD, along with a set of abilities and qualities that, with the right support and guidance, can result in amazing accomplishments. The frequency and typical symptoms of ADHD in boys, diagnosis and evaluation, fostering a supportive home environment, developing routines, and defining reasonable expectations have all been covered in this book. We've also discussed dealing with schools, creating tailored education plans, diet and nutrition, behavioral therapy, alternative treatments, and sleep and exercise.

Additionally, we have addressed anxiety and depression, taught coping skills, developed social awareness, made friends, handled bullying and peer pressure, supported positive relationships, managed impulsivity, dealt with frustration and anger, built self-esteem, and covered a number of other crucial topics. The particular difficulties associated with adolescence, hormonal changes, and the transition to middle and high school have also been covered.

The significance of self-advocacy, career exploration, ongoing education, medication management, and skill development has been emphasized as adults with ADHD approach adulthood. They will benefit greatly from having tenacity and patience on this path.

This guide's fundamental message is one of empowerment and hope. People with ADHD can reach their full potential and have happy lives by appreciating their accomplishments, valuing self-care, and maintaining an optimistic outlook on the future. Even though the route has many turns and turns, it is still worthwhile.

In conclusion, overcoming ADHD with fortitude and resilience is evidence of the extraordinary abilities of people with ADHD and the resolute support of their loved ones, teachers, and medical professionals. This manual functions as a road map, providing direction and support at each turn. As we come to an end, let us keep in mind that the future is bright for people with ADHD if they have the appropriate approaches, perseverance, and patience.

www.ingramcontent.com/pod-product-compliance
Lightning Source LLC
Chambersburg PA
CBHW070808260726
48660CB00005B/1765